Tesserae

"Anyone who has lived with lifelong grief knows the storms, fissures, and caverns it can erupt in our lives, some of which promise to wash us away before we can climb out of them. Michelle McLean knows this feeling of drowning on dry land all too well and has created a beautifully wrought collection of poems that have both tormented her and brought her a form of catharsis. By sharing these remarkable and also ordinary moments around her sister's untimely death and the aftermath, we get to hold space with her as she struggles for purchase and are relieved to find her exhausted but alive on the other side. It's never easy being the one who lived."

Jenn Carson
author and director of the L.P. Fisher Public Library

"The poems of *Tesserae* take the reader skilfully from a place of despair and regret through an awakening where new life and light grow from past tragedy. The poet shows how truth and fortitude can lead through darkness to a place where love and memory combine to create a new understanding of life and living."

Jane Tims
author of *mnemonic: soundscape and birdsong*

"I have walked this road with Michelle and I love how she has set and solved her poetic puzzles. I hope everybody enjoys her journey as much as I have."

Roger Moore
Professor Emeritus
St. Thomas University

Tesserae

Poems by
Michelle McLean

Chapel Street Editions

Appreciation of Place

Chapel Street Editions exists within the unceded and unsurrendered territories of the Wolastoqiyik, Mi'kmaq, and Peskotomuhkati people. The work we do is born from the stories carried by this land and its inhabitants. The animals, plants, soil, water, and air make this place home for the Indigenous people who belong to this land, for the descendants of those who took this land and made it a belonging, and for those who have since come from away. Chapel Street Editions holds a deep appreciation for our place within this land and the stories it tells. We honour the land's Indigenous caretakers and are grateful for their wisdom and guidance.

© Copyright 2024 Michelle McLean
All right reserved

Published by
Chapel Street Editions
150 Chapel St. Woodstock, NB Canada E7M 1H4
chapelstreeteditions@gmail.com
www.chapelstreeteditions.com

ISBN 978-1-988299-54-9

Library and Archives Canada Cataloguing in Publication

Title: Tesserae / poems by Michelle McLean.
Other titles: Tesserae (Compilation)
Names: McLean, Michelle, 1975- author.
Identifiers: Canadiana 20240357671 | ISBN 9781988299549 (softcover)
Subjects: LCGFT: Poetry.
Classification: LCC PS8625.L4293 T47 2024 | DDC C811/.6—dc23

Book design by Brendan Helmuth

Cover design by Kayte McLaughlin

Dedication

In loving memory of my sister, Tracey Lynne McLean (1972-1987)
I love and miss you, always.

And for my mother, for holding up the sky.

Table of Contents

Owning our story and loving ourselves through that process is the bravest thing that we will ever do.

Brené Brown *The Gifts of Imperfection*

Preface

Poetry has always been a dear friend to me. Reading and writing poetry have been both a compulsion and a healing force throughout my life. *Tesserae* is about finding beauty in the broken, inspired in part by *Kintsukuroi,* the Japanese art of repairing broken pottery with lacquer mixed with powdered gold, silver or platinum. I am drawn to its philosophy of treating breakage and repair as part of the history of an object, rather than something to disguise or discard.

Tesserae explores both what is shattered, and what we seek to rebuild. It's about reclaiming, repurposing, integrating, and sometimes, letting go. It's about the quest for narrative cohesion, piecing together the orphaned fragments of our lives, our loves, our losses, and our sense of self.

When I was twelve years old, my family was shattered in ways that have never been repaired. My sister Tracey was killed in a horrific accident. She was fifteen. My sister was my idol, my competitor, my playmate; she was my confidante, my co-conspirator, my hero, my tormentor, my protector. She was my mentor and my witness. *Tesserae* traces the journey of trauma, grief, addiction and recovery. It is equal parts scream and lullaby.

Trauma changes the brain—a consequence compounded by the often unhelpful ways one seeks to cope with trauma. Recovery alters the brain as well. Writing these poems has helped me take command of my pain, and to have compassion for the child and the young woman who was doing her best to navigate that suffering. For most of my life, I believed I was unequivocally and irrevocably broken—a belief that spawned cumulatively painful consequences. I didn't realize I could feel differently, that healing was possible. Tragically, I've known and loved many beautiful souls who also feel this way. I want them to know this "brokenness", this sense of defectiveness, is a toxic lie. No matter how deeply rooted these beliefs may be, it doesn't make them true. Healing and recovery are possible. We all deserve this gift. In some ways, these poems are love letters to younger parts of myself. They are love letters to anyone who feels broken, unlovable, or alone. We are none of these things. We can let in the light. We *are* the light.

Crash

Retrospective

A sin, really, our pranks at the lake
teasing Mom with our underwater prowess

Hand to her throat
she paced the shore
waiting for us to surface

Breathless, we emerged
giddy and giggling

neither of us dreaming
we were mortal

Imaginary Lines

If only you knew the picture
you made at the front of the room
a face that brought grown men
to their knees

You didn't plan this event
not your fault
it was such a bleak affair

Great turn out, though

I still remember the gut flutter
warning

> *Look*
> *but don't touch*
> *touching might be*
> *too much*
> *could crack you*
> *like a nut*

But something compelled
my hand to your cheek
cold and hard as the brook stones
we used to cut the devil's throat

Lips sealed, like mine
would become

this shall not pass

Chicken Little

Eyes so wide
pinball antics front to back

        to side
to side

                lost

in the vast unknown
thrown for a loop
fumbling the drift

    can't bridge the rift

What happens now? she screams inside
Should I run, take cover?
Should I hide?

No acorns and no answers here

fear drives longing
for her mother's arms
soft and warm
torn
by silent questions

What happens now?
What happened?

Why?

She can't see you, little one

    Mama's holding up the sky

Etymology

Wake *Waeccan*
Old English for
staying with the body

It was a job in those days;
people were hired.

No mention of the cost

Tesserae

You are part of all parts of me
my smooth surfaces, sharp sides
convince me
broken is still beautiful

Our shared and unshared childhoods
our family detonated
fragments
pulled toward the same darkness
that swallowed our father whole

Convince me
it will be okay
you could hold my daughters' faces
in your hands
like robin's eggs
weave daisy chains around our hearts

Convince me
broken is still beautiful

I have so much to tell you
so much to ask
my voice, echoing

What would you make of this mosaic of mine?
Can you trace your hands
across its story,
feel its prayer?

Convince me
there is beauty in
shrapnel
held
to the light

Keepsakes

Your absence makes the heart grow
in mysterious ways

the house itself turns traitor
walls talking
furniture mocking

Your vacant chair
at the kitchen table
emptied another –
its owner, unable to accept
our remaining trinity
as his personal saviour

Taunted by what remains
proportional distortions
the cedar chest that
swallowed your room

hungry mouth of memory
consuming
what little is left

So much holding

Even your clock stopped

> *you always had a flair*
> *for the dramatic!*

Some took this literally
spent years killing time

Unequal to the sad, slow task
of taking down the shrine

Thursday's Child

I still remember the costumes
you were eight, I was five

A wee Lucifer, shoulder-hunched
and anvil heavy, watching you twirl
resplendent in a gown of golden satin
recycled from a wedding

Glittered, star-topped wand
like Glinda, *the good witch*

My crimson cape (perfect for
dramatic entrances)
was custom-made
I tried to feel grateful
resisting the urge to poke you
with my plywood pitchfork
hot tears behind my beastly
plastic mask

No more pictures now
it's taken me years to find
some sympathy
for this little devil
to recognize that sometimes
it's the monster
needing rescue

not the princess

Leaves

I remember you collecting them
for a science project
carefully pressed
in an album
labeled in pink, loopy cursive
I would later emulate

Butternut, Birch,
Oak, Beech

Your favourite, one
of only two leaves
on our father's fledgling
red maple
plucked without permission
much too young
for this severing
stunted its growth

Like these leaves
we're not as you left us

We're more brittle now
curling in at the edges
guarding our hearts
fearful
they might crumble

to the touch

My Sister, My Keeper

1

The clementine oranges
you slipped into my room
one night I was sent to bed
without supper
for some now-forgotten crime
their clandestine sweetness
the delight
of your risk
the way you held my hand
wiped my tears
whispered

It's not your fault

2

You ditched your friends at the fair
finding me fear-frozen
at the barred window
of the *House of Horrors*
unable to budge from the only
slice of light

Without scolding or complaint,
you eased my clammy hands
from iron bars
guided me through dark
narrow passage of
shabby, backlit ghouls

3

You, standing sky-high
bullet-proof
over the girl who
never taunted me again
fist in the face of her spluttering
disclaimers
one ominous word

don't

4

The way you knew things
children shouldn't know
assumed I was wise enough
to understand
made sure I steered clear of the man
with the mind full of grime
and the mouth full of God

5

I try not to think about it
the truck slamming like a clenched fist
into the face of the water

The guardrail came too late

Catch and Release

Memory doesn't keep
its appointments with me
shows up unannounced
coaxing me to make time with ghosts

Rainscent
summers at the camp
catching crayfish
multitudes scavenged
from the stream
no stone unturned
such pride in our bounty
their frantic gratitude
when set free

* * *

Salamander stalking
tricky to find,
harder to hold

Stealth slide under the step
feline vigilance
bragging rights sealed
with tickle-flutter
in my closed fist

* * *

Kaleidoscope of minnows
in our plastic buckets

Scent of moss — petrichor
wet stones
your *double-dog-dare-you* eyes
as we spin on inner tubes
hot from the sun

The place where I most
felt our family whole
sold
after you left us
to dam up the flooding
of memory

we flounder
treading water

Good Girl

Restless tongue twitching
in dark cave of mouth
baby tooth loose
blood basted
gnawed raw

I fear a mess
is imminent, a scene
lurking behind the
crimson curtain
of my smile

Heart hammering
mercury rising
I turn the other cheek
ending the business
with a yank

Hide it in a napkin
in the safety of my room
tuck it under my pillow

wait for change

Thy Perfect Light

The house, heavy with its feast
of tragedy and time
unbuttoned with a sigh

Belly full of grief, it hunkered down
for sleep but we still haunted it

> *Make me in thine image;*
> *make me to hear joy and gladness,*
> *that the bones which Thou hast broken*
> *may rejoice*

I betrayed us both
hallowing thy name
trying to slide into
your skin
heart consumed
by the weight
of all you might have been

I tried on your clothes
beat myself with your bones
unable to quiet the voice in my ear
the face making faces
in the mirror

It's taken years for me
to cup my hands around a prayer
hold it to my lips
give thanks
years to forgive the girl
who longed to walk a mile
in your dancing shoes
bumbling her way through
the wreckage

still finding her feet

Refractions

Your love, a mirror

                 carnival glass

     I've tantrum smashed

                      a thousand times inside

fragments catching light

             burning holes

             through the worn fabric

of my hopes for change

            I wasn't always like this, you know

jagged sharp

             shards in the heart

how you left us

         without leaving

              the drawn drapes in your room

       dark womb

where you weave a shroud of the past

                  my arms, unable to encircle

     your grief

         hang restless for rescue

nothing to do

              but turn a kind eye

      mind the edges of this love

          ensure its safe storage

Degrees of Separation

At fifteen
I didn't know much
about babies
but I knew they shouldn't
be blue as an azure sky.

Do you still carry
those pictures with you
as I carry them with me?
Or did you shed them, with time,
finding the collection too heavy?

I wish I had known what to say,
straitjacketed behind the checkout
in my orange and navy apron,
clutching your pot roast
like a shield
that could somehow protect me
from what had been offered,
something I had no language
to name.

My tongue turned to stone with your
china doll smile and dark river eyes
as I watched you carefully return
the photos to your purse.

Isn't he beautiful?
You said

Yes

I think I said

He is.

You Can't Get There from Here

Spent the afternoon
nursing a cocktail
of what I want to say
then swallowed it down
1 part longing
2 parts memory

Transported
to lazy summer Sundays
the Land Rover belch bumbling
over backroads
as you try to teach me
to drive a stick shift

Whistling tunes that never
reached those haunted eyes
a world we could no longer enter

Wary, wistful
you wonder aloud
how many more trips
are left in the old beast

First and reverse are the trickiest,
you say

I can't find the proper gear
to manage this terrain
your pain stifling my plea
bullying my resolve

Lost again on this familiar ground
unable to navigate
this rickety mass of feeling
to guide my words
toward the dusty road
of redemption

Keenan Bridge

We drove out that afternoon
with a full case of beer
and a gut full of grief
bumbling our way through
feelings we dared not speak.

I remember how the forest floor
embroidered our skin
while we slapped down
mosquitoes the size of dimes.

Our bodies, brailled with chill,
spoke to one another in language
we both understood
when little else made sense.

Sharp blade of moon bearing witness
to the long walk home.

Grief is a Shape Shifter

Sitting dock's end
at sunset
dipping its toe
tracing water
scanning horizon for answers
that never come

Like a seagull
thieving any scraps of joy
it can find
a miserable, noisy thug
shitting on the parked cars
of our carefully laid plans

Stealthily folding into itself
like a secret it was told
to keep as a child
a snake coiled tight
in the throat,
waiting to strike

The unwanted jigsaw puzzle
you got for Christmas
a thousand pieces
of *full-on forest*

A ladder against the window
beckoning me outside past curfew,
initiating all kinds of trouble

The drunkest girl at the party
needy, inexplicably indignant
demanding over and over
that you play her song

A house engulfed in flames
no insurance

Submersion

Via Negativa

being lost,
being crazy maybe
is not so bad
if you can be
that way
undisturbed.

Charles Bukowski
"Young in New Orleans"

Rats in the woodwork
long aware
of human disease
seek shelter

When silence descends
so does the smell

The moon howls at the wolf
full knowing who is truly big and bad
around here

Following her call
into thick, dark night
bestial beauty
soaking my senses
as I bide my time
against the ragged earth

answering
to no one

Caveat

As children we are told
there are no monsters
under the bed.

Perhaps true,
but sometimes they're on top.
They make you believe in them —
make-believe
black magic mind.

Sunday Night Bingo

All grief, anyone's grief,
is the weight of a sleeping child

Anne Michaels
Fugitive Pieces

Your firstborn sleeps eternal
a whisper in the ear
a bundle swaddled
at the bottom of the breath

I, alone, am the promise
the fountain of youth
the only ovaries left
all the eggs in one
basket-case who tosses back *Fireball*
in the toilet stall
of the Kinsmen, while you
organize sheets, situate charms

Each clinging to our rituals
of comfort
our gimmicks
for chasing down luck

I grow careless
with my numbers
uninvested in the cards
I've been dealt

Oblivious
omnipotent,
the bearded caller
continues

I sense without looking
your eyes over my shoulder
searching, as always,
for what I may have missed

Having learned in the most
harrowing way
life is a gamble
giving yourself
to games of chance
committed to beating odds

chasing jackpots

Requiem for a Scale

Years ago, you pitched it
into the field behind our house
like a barroom bouncer
turfing a troublemaker
exiled forever from our bathroom

I haven't had one since

I still remember
how we looked at each other
almost shyly, a touch afraid
then laughed the moment
down to the floor
leaving me
breathless, thankful

a little wiser
than before

Feral

The words I should have said
turned themselves in circles
then curled up trembling
in my throat

I beat them down
sent them away
now I can't coax them out
when I need them
they won't be fooled
by my iron-on smile
faux friendly voice
promising food

They're hiding in the junkyard
of unspoken syllables
but if you get close enough
you can hear them snarling

Placebo

Tying you tightly around me
to stop the bleeding, too late
discovering the limits
of strongarm tactics

Mainlining desire
like a sacred elixir
like an *answer*
you were flattered
to be my mood-altering
substance

Our love is snake oil
sold on every corner
no prescription for peace
it's a silver bullet
that won't bring down the
beast

From *Notes to Self*

Joni Mitchell offered this —

> *Smile pretty and watch your back*

Wise advice,
for a sleeve-worn heart
takes inevitable beatings
it bleeds
picks up lint
pumps out messes
in unfortunate places

Still, I can't tuck it away
can't make it mind
my warnings
not to give candy
to strangers

Scavenger Hunt

Lips, two, on a pirate's neck
hair spooled around a fist
like thread; both eyes flown
to the back of your head

Your foot under the bed
where you've kept it for luck
grounding the wire
to charm off the howling
and breathing of fire

But where is the heart?
Poor, sick, bloated beast

Hidden safely away
and frozen,
at least

Adaptation

She loves with a chip on her shoulder
makes an art of indifference
my insomnia sidekick
nocturnal familiar

She tolerates my ticking clock
as I maul her with kisses
and baby talk, cootchie cooing her
into a feral rage

She's taught me about priorities
Sappho can always find a slice of sun
to chase around the house

She's relentless in this quest
willing to destroy
knocks away all knick knacks
to clear a space
for warmth
and light

Passenger Side

Ella's singing *Summertime*
and the livin' is easy

> I want so badly
> to believe her

From behind funky sunglasses
and ridiculous hats
I watched you fall for
my fetching disguise

and I, hungry for something
yet unnamed, disappeared
into your soft, blind eyes

Visiting Hours

The lingering image of your hands
like startled ants, flying restless
for a place to settle
I think of all they've cradled and created
what a malignant cheat life can be

I grope for words
mind frantically scanning
its chapters for some offering
something to make you smile

Instead, I'm struck mute
transfixed by your hands
remembering how they carried
the duties of the day, defying migraines
that would bring most to their knees

They've performed miracles
held and raised your children
their calm competence always knowing
what the moment required;
hands well-seasoned in giving
though shrinking to receive

Each summer, harvesting forgotten vegetables
from my mother's refrigerator
with lamentations of waste

Powerless over this cellular invasion
this thief that's hijacked your body
I'm robbed of words
thoughts rooting with the Swedish Ivy
your daughter labours compulsively
to propagate
cuttings covering every available surface
in her home like a second skin

Wishing I could turn back time
comforts of denial peeled away
like the gelatinous skin of hospital desserts

I made a promise to myself that day
I'm still trying to keep –
to somehow find my way out of the waiting room

To honour, as you have, the treasure of this life
knowing it's in my hands

Lakeside Distillations

Porch swing metronome
pacing the heart
brazen hummingbirds
dive bomb feeders
lunging as we linger
wine-sleepy over
tacit bonds of

just one more

We, too, hover for our nectar

Summer yawns, ready for its nap
we speak of departures, arrivals
strange places where lives collide

Tangerine sky
canopies wistful water
sighing softly toward shore
your hand on my leg
hesitant, now

We speak of changes
seasons winding down
scanning the horizon for
a different ending
beyond the bloodshot eye
of the setting sun

Happy Hour

Do I not feel the hunger so acutely
that I would rather die
than look into its face?

> Anne Sexton
> "Cigarettes and Whiskey and Wild, Wild Women"

Girl on a stool
bird on a wire
thirst for drink
quest for fire

Battered will
hogtied brain
play the song, Sam
please
again

Last call
brick wall—
searching the softest place
to fall

Throats and tables
being cleared
ashtrays emptied

Can't stay here

Holding her face
like worry stone
facing the evening
on her own
is not at all what she had
in mind

I have been her kind

Rigor Mortis

We spend the day steeped in death
stench and labour transformed
to sustenance
a winter's worth of meals
for the freezer

Piles of glazed eyes watch as
we butcher, scald, and pluck our way
through the afternoon's silent arguments
holding our breath
soiling our hands

At day's end
we share a sink, small talk
work up enough lather
to break the surface tension
almost enough
to wash us clean

Darkness descends
our hands transition to work
that feels just as final
I consider the nuances of touch
the various methods of bleeding out life

All that we do in the name of hunger

calling it humane

Denouement

On Valentine's Day
I packed my things
morning quiet as a corpse

While you invented chores
in the yard
my friends ploughed up in pickups
helping remove all evidence
of my presence, as though
from a crime scene

In the rear-view mirror
the cottage sits like an accusation
I consider my perennials
that cluttered your landscape
thinking of bulbs
spring will bring to life
memories blooming
when least expected

Scattered seeds, looking to root
bearing witness
to how hard we tried

Epiphanophobia

The truth fairy's accustomed
to a bit of blood
she comes at night
before the oblivion of sleep
leaving whispers
under my pillow

>   *wake up,*
>   *I have something*
>   *to show you*

It's no fun
rousing the mind
from sleep
like a surly drunk
crashed on the couch
it rages resistance
slaps the snooze
calls in sick

just itching for a fight

Vertigo

Never again
comes sooner than planned
long before never
I'm stirring it up
staring it down
bravado burning my throat

I bless myself with unholy water
say a prayer, light a candle;
ritual has its comforts

        though sometimes flammable

Living it up is easy
it's the living down
existential hangover
that tells me this show
can't go on

In a certain slant of light
my shadow is bigger than me
one part lover, three parts fiend
it carries me home by the hair,
puts me to bed
whispers endearments
chokes my little chicken neck
then draws me close

for feeding

Precious Metals

I don't know why they call them
golden years, you said

I consider aging
bruising like fruit
ripening from the inside out

Dreading the day my teeth
adorn the bedside table
sidekick to my jewellery

Watching my body betray me
intestine and bowel getting lippy
disrespecting rules and routines
attempts at discipline; mere movement
requires caution, equipment

I stand in the doorway to your room
vanilla milkshake sweating in my hand
trying to prepare myself for the eyes
you might be wearing today –
restless, glazed, frantic?

Perhaps today, they will be your own

Rooting my thoughts in the days
before the edges of your mind began to curl
I remember the tanned furrows
of your summer skin
like tractor-combed fields

Pulling pictures from the rich soil
of your life sustains me
through these incoherent afternoons

I think of your gardens
your mastery of the landscape
hands deep in the dark earth

Is it wrong that I want you
to *go gentle into that good night*
like pollen into the air?

I sit on the edge of your bed
knowing I'm too late to thank you
for all you've taught me

Golden is the silence of memory
built to outlast the body's welcome
transcending time's indignities
enduring
well worth the keeping

Daily Bread

Still learning to navigate the space
between duty and desire
altruism and appetite
I watch you pull fresh loaves from the oven
knuckles like the tips of bone china
body curled into itself
as though to embrace
all it has contained

Ravaged eyesight
you go by feel, instinct
adaptive artistry that helps me believe
I, too, can rise –
apprentice to the possibility of
sated hunger
trespasses forgiven

abundance carried
in trembling hands

Negative Space

Unsettling to wake in a stranger's bed
finding it's your own
splayed open, frayed at the edges
a toothbrush past its prime
sweaty palm of reckoning
reaching in the dark
hand on my knee
wondering how far this can go

When life is an abusive lover
I cling to my symbols
mnemonics of survival

If the heart could speak
it would be a baby's wail
in an empty room

Echoing

* * *

Brain's on a bender
can't see the big picture
gestalt faces
the old, the young woman
one and the same

Inside out, my seams
unseemly
mind blown open
a screen door in the wind

* * *

I know this swan song by heart
dropped at the door with a squeeze on the arm
a forehead kiss
an illusion, this dignified parting
there must be more
much, much more

When the spinning's stopped, I'll pour another
to stave off the dry heave of regret
almost able to convince myself
that everyone
gets their fifteen minutes
of shame

* * *

Rage has been bundled and rocked
but won't stay down
stretch marks of the past chart the birth
of something new and strange
no cherub cheeked promise
of a fresh start
but something I can't yet claim
or name

The truth is no toy
small parts pose a choking hazard

Swaddled but unsoothed
wide eyed in white noise, yearning
pain in my gut, fist in my mouth
no words to articulate
this hunger

* * *

I overpacked for this trip through time
too much baggage
wandering my way through
moth-mauled memory
like a stray dog
that will take its shelter anywhere,
wary, but grateful

Memory shaped by the beast that beats
you can dress it up, take it out
but no guarantees
it will behave itself

Trembling, hand to the door
dust motes in the air
this is what it is to be haunted

but no longer spooked

        * * *

The longing, a collect call at 3 a.m.
knowing I'll accept the charges
illusions, confusions abound
while stewing the bones of the past
lifting the lid
the stench overpowers

The soul has something up its sleeve,
pulls a plan from behind my ear

       Abracadabra
       Alacazam!

For my next trick

       watch me disappear

Mental Health Waiting Room

Amongst the ribs and dust
in this forgotten garden
kindness reveals itself
in the most unlikely places

Jesus in blue jeans
Newsweek on his lap
wants to bathe my wounds
with his tears
I can see it in his eyes
he knows what it is
to suffer, forsaken
to face annihilation
with a mannequin smile
and a throat full of thunder

To Be Continued

Time, deadbeat roommate
ducked out of last month's rent
left behind its belongings for me
to deal with, will someday call
and ask to split the damage deposit
like nothing happened

* * *

Open Meeting of the minds
they've got me over a cracker barrel
mind cluttered with platitudes
and fresh out of good news

Fake it till you make it
they say, but neglect to tell me
what to do with this ire, this fire
whiskey warm in my throat

I tried to shake it off
but took a chill

Mouth giving thanks
brain shooting blanks
wondering how long it will be
this time
before I'm finished
wadding snot-stained tissue
into little pockets of peace

* * *

Confessions, voodoo
picked apart
vultures circling my bones
soon you'll be able to tell fortunes
give advice with what's left of me
shake me out of a sack
warn others

* * *

The will is wearing its work clothes
no patience for pleasantries
rolling up its sleeves for the dirty work ahead
working lost ground
with a dull spade

Dig deeply enough anywhere
you'll find something
in some stage of rot

Trying to find stillness
chasing sleep that can't be found
amidst the sound of beaks
piercing the crust
of another new beginning

* * *

Wanted: Heavy duty brainwash
for stubborn stains

Nothing too abrasive
no stifling floral scent

no residue

* * *

There's a pair of ragged claws
scuttling under my skin
as I sit doing time in my mind
unsure whether to fly
or lay an egg

I grow older
I grow older
Self-talk growing sassy
bolder

Do I dare disturb the universe?
I wish I may, I wish I might
win this fight
or go down swinging

* * *

My feelings embarrass me these days
I pretend not to know them
when they drop me off
pick me up
I don't know how they can be so
painfully square, so unaware
of the unseasoned words
I burn inside

the threat of fire in the throat

* * *

Curiosity tests the contours
of my better judgment
scratch and win, nails digging
into the soft flesh of my resolve
inching around the chalk lines
of my best intentions
you wash your hands with a sigh

suits me

Longing to be forgotten
like cheap sandals on the beach

* * *

I want to shape the wisdom
of the ages
into a big black ball
knock down all my pretty little pins

start over
start smarter

* * *

Hope stops getting dressed
hardly leaves the house
needs reminders to bathe

Hiding too long in ditches
roadkill shadows
gnawing off limbs caught
in the same old traps
making my way to the coarse
red meat of the matter
dressing wounds of another year spent
trying too hard

* * *

Conjugal visit to the prison mind
locust-swarm memories find me
thumbing the pages of my dogeared dreams
tired of repairing a heart
that keeps breaking in the same places

Piñata brain, bludgeoned awake
feeling superfluous as a toaster cozy
a leaf pressed between the pages
of a book that will never be read

Surrounded by soothesayers
with their kind lies

you can do this, girl
you got this

It seems impossible
like hopscotch on stilts

They hold the faith
for safe keeping
until I have the courage
to carry it home

* * *

The heart signed no living will
wants heroic measures taken
turns off the death support
ready to flex its muscle, keep beat
with the rhythm of possibility

knowing neither tune nor words

tries to sing

* * *

The truth is only one side of the story
here's the chaser—

It's a long way down
to the place where we meet
our deepest wounds

to the space where we kneel
and heal

Note to self

You don't have to lie in the bed
you've made
if it's lumpy, holding sleep hostage

Be careful what you allow to curl up
on the mind's memory foam

No one has the last word on you

we're each of us, every one,

slightly askew

A La Carte

You only ate my heart out because
I set it on a plate before you
beaming as you polished off each bite
sopping up the juices of my best intentions
with a piece of day-old bread

A novice cook, I underestimated
the feast required, panicked
when you asked for seconds

scrambling through cupboards,
clawing my way through old recipes
stirring up dust

Hoping to find something
to appease your hunger
my own stomach growling
like a cornered animal
I toss and toil
bringing my rage to a strong
slow boil

My cup runneth empty
though you say
you still want something sweet
tonight, I suggest dining out

this time, your treat

Cruelest Month

This year, the brute black boot
of winter went straight for the head
kicking while I was down
December fought dirty

April finds me unkempt, unruly
with new life, restless for colour
I welcome green in all its forms
perhaps unwisely—
Spring can be tricky
in this secret garden
hard to tell beauty from beast

I understand how roots
can be held hostage
and why it's hard, sometimes,
to bloom where you're planted

I did research
Attracting Beneficials
Butterflies

Wary of creepers
that bully the landscape
crowding out climbers
stretch-searching their path
toward the light
of the sun

Unprepared
for what bursts from the earth
hardy, stubborn
demanding attention
invasives that threaten
to choke out the bloom

I've tried chemicals
but the cost is high

I'm learning
to respect nature

Fine Print

This part holds her longings
secret and close
like a high school love note
tucked in her bra

But such hiding
leaves creases
lines become blurred

Living so long by rote
she never imagined forgetting

It's amazing
what a few years
a few fears can do
when the past we cradle and curse
grows claws and jaws
fills malnourished hope
with a new kind
of hunger

When I See Her From Here

I wonder how there can be so much she doesn't know. I cringe
watching her hustle for approval and affection like some carnival act
backed into a corner of her own making, taking any available shelter
from awareness of her pain—that stubborn, stubborn stain.

Seeking love in strange places, lost in all the wrong faces but unable
to look in the mirror.

When I see her from here, I watch how she runs so hard and so fast
from anything that might last, in terror she would never name.
All the same, I understand when I see her from here.

I understand her disconnected fear, the optical delusions
of the unhealed heart. I start to know her in a different way;
I want to tell her *it will be okay,* that even when it isn't,
this too, shall pass. *Girl, have some class.*

When I see her from here, I feel a lump in my throat filled
with all the things I want her to say, the voice I want her to own.
I want her to know what's at stake, to fight raw *red in tooth and claw*
but know too, when to surrender.

I want to shake her to her core beliefs, those thieves
that keep her frightened and small and tell her,
"You're writing the script, acting the roles—you're doing it all
girl, and you don't even know."

When I see her from here, I want to help her steer, to sidestep
those illusions, confusions that have taken her down, down
and back around so many times. Retrying the same old crimes.

I want to tell her, "Don't let the creases set on your perspective,
especially without a *vision*; no division of body and mind.
Don't abandon what carries you home. *You are not alone.*"

When I see her from here, I'm not sure whether to give her a hug or a hammer. I want to tell her there are worse things in this world than being lost. I want to warn her of the cost of chemical escape. I want to hand her that flying cape. I want to scream *Watch Out!* for that hole, that pole, that tortured soul.

Tell her the only life she can save is her own.

Evidence of Surfacing

Speak

Silence has its own violence
the bruises of unspokens
getting tricky to conceal
I'm through walking into every door
I seek to open
lost in illusions, fingers crossed
with my signals

all the room's elephants
balanced on my chest

Silence is a bully
ignoring won't send it away

Sometimes, when we're alone
the truth begins to unbutton
shows a little skin
shy, but not unwilling

I'm ready

I've singed a few bridges,
had to find alternate routes
without a map
but I'm not lost

We've had a good run, shame
but I've had enough
you chafe

I open to the words trapped
in my throat,
pull them forth
like magician scarves
paint the sky
with a new story

In *Medias Res*

You dropped my name and it broke
on the floor

trying to make sense
of this ragged, shattered scene

all the spaces in between with your
fingerprints wiped clean

Sharp edges of my pain
warn, *handle with care*
thin skin
beware

I will not throw away
this tesserae
I've never been one for waste
(though I like things
properly spaced)

I've been long collecting
for this mosaic
pulling in, sifting out

Still arranging

no plans, as yet
to grout

Survival Tips

1

When fear has you cornered,
teeth bared and fur bristled,
know this —

only its master
can call it off

2

Guilt is a grisly affair
hang around too long
and it's bound to take you down

The scat is your warning
don't wait for the roaring

Hold fast to your wits
if caught, you'll be mauled
to the bone

Just its nature

No use hiding
it will find you out
having tracked your scent

Your best options —
avoid, or amend

It beats playing dead

3

Rage, unjustly curfewed
grounded
finds a way of sneaking out

has a whole life you're unaware of
beyond the reconnaissance
of dreams

Stealthy at first
ear to the ground
it grows increasingly
rebellious, careless
with growing appetite

Anything could happen

Without proper guidance
it shacks up with fear
spawns chaos that can't be swaddled
a heart that won't be soothed
by any amount of rocking

4

Tears born of grief
are distinct from other tears –
those coaxed by allergies
dirt in the eye

Their chemical composition
holds different proteins
slow release
the sting, more forgiving

They know where they've come from
they don't deny their roots

They have something to say
in the still-point quiet
of surrender

our purpose is
to cleanse

From *Notes to Self II*

Geese overhead
bump-feathered your skin
from leavened head
to leaden feet

As you considered arrivals
departures
your thoughts migrated south,
restless for warmth

Time left behind its luggage
weighed down watching
dreams stop for coffee
at the border of conviction
waiting for courage
to cross

You, too, are waiting
thinking of all the places
you could be, considering
all your paths, your props
and your best laid plans
blowing smoke
at the sign that clearly reads

You are here

You are the Ocean

People who live by the sea,
understand eternity

Erica Jong
"People Who Live"

Vast, unknown depths
never emptied or absorbed

Life dumped its pollution
its epic demands
but your tidal heart
attuned to ebb and flow
whims of weather
offered no submission

Holding grief's dense salinity
many times over
still brimming with life
taking in, letting go

Unifying tributaries, currents of our lives
with the rhythm of one at home in natural law

Awed by your strength and spirit
the travellers you've carried—
daily artistry of endurance
adaptation

Undulating waves softening
sharp edges of glass and stone
washed back to our shores
your bounty, boundless

Perhaps why many of us
have become beachcombers
collectors of treasure
daily reminders to train the eye
for beauty, solace

You are the ocean
part of all you have touched,
all that has touched you
across infinite distance with timeless voice
a legacy of life

symphony of waves

From *Notes to Self III*

You've spent years
dragging yourself
across jagged edges
and rough surfaces
to exfoliate dead skin
of the past

Taken apart
your torn, tattered heart
still beats

Take a minute
do the math
the long division of pain
and payoff

Note the remainder

Listen to the voice inside—
a hymn
singing soft and slow

Come In

Higher Learning

I found the shoebox nestled
in the dark of my closet
amongst spurned textbooks
juvenilia
and my funeral pumps

It took a moment to recognize
the man I'd made metaphor
who sent mail faithfully
while I dragged my burdened brain
(kicking and screaming)
through university

Notecards of chickadees, teddy bears
with goofy free-hand drawings
mark years spent scanning
footnotes for an answer
to *why the caged bird sings*
when I can't choke out a note

Always a little money tucked inside
like a secret

Dust collects in corners we don't often visit
settles itself without ceremony
waiting for us to pay attention
to the names written across
the neglected surfaces of our past

waiting to be read aloud

Preteen Triptych

1

Bubblegum-pink painted toenails
makeover madness
acid wash warriors
cashmere queens
you let me mess with your makeup
(even took some tips from me)
then filled our bathroom sink
to uncover the mystery and magic
of *Tampax*
blowing my mind
in this strange new form

2

The bicycle you kept under your window
for late night escapes
escapades
I kept your secret,
even from you

gut bomb
ready to detonate

3

Love's Baby Soft blankets
the room as you lip sync
to George Michael
your body, like water
the way you tossed your hair, winked
and blew me a kiss
entrenching my life-long heroine addiction

I keep it on my playlist
for times of need

'cause I gotta have faith

Lady Bonsai

Trick-clipped
into shapes her nature
never intended

Your pruning
economical love
leaving no room for error
no wasted space
small enough to fit
in the palm of your hand

Soon tiring
of this forced precision
tamed periphery
she uprooted

grew her way back
to the wild

Gardening Notes

I couldn't clear the landfill
of my mind
by recycling the past
I had to break it down

Rake piling grief, regret
longing, well-watered
seeds unfit for planting
peelings of skin I've shed

Ancient rage, brittle betrayals
crumbled in my fists
fears blown free
on opening palms to the wind

The turning over
again
and again

A wonder to witness
this wasteland
slowly transformed
to fertile possibility
goes to show, you never can tell
where help might come from
what form grace will take
eluding the naked eye,
doing dirty work unseen

I yield to the wisdom of the earth
and breathe

This Side Up

I'm difficult, inconsistent
live beyond my means
take uncalculated risks
ignore sound advice
nap in inappropriate places
sometimes bite
the hand that strokes me

I've been careless, dabbled in love
buried wounds in need of tending
for a bottle of merlot
I'll show you where it hurts

I have a history
of being in the right place
at the wrong time
play our song backwards
and the lyrics might offend

Why our love
sometimes chafes
keeps me up at night
when stone age fears
and knuckle dragging notions
won't surrender to
the circadian rhythm of
this new condition
when nothing can quiet
the bones beneath the breath

I press a prayer to my lips
strap in for the ride
make my wishes from this point on
with eyes open wide

       wide
           wide

Roadside Assistance

Things happen when body and mind
go their separate ways
citing irreconcilable differences
every time I turn around
something's breaking down

I'm mostly considered for parts
these days
I trust my mechanic
but no guarantees for the work
I'm reading my manuals
learning "how tos"
trying not to bruise

yet to fully own what carries me
but steadily making payments

Natural Habitats

Limbs entwined, double helix
under rumpled sheets as the bunkhouse creaks
with wind pulled up from the Strait

Night swim shivers, keeping beat
our body heat cradling the cold as we lie thankful
under the spilled light of the moon

My head rests easy on your heart
hand snail curled under chin, our thoughts
nestled in warm pockets of the evening
while your hands play through my hair
as though still searching water

Head full of dreams and a crush on the world
you say my name like you mean it
as I rock you to sleep with the song of my skin

Second Skin

Deciding, finally
to settle down
rests more comfortably
against my bones
but still has its regressions
transgressions
trysts with despair
the holding of breath

Your hand on mine
anchoring the moment
tracing thread veins
along my skin
spooling the heart

Soft applause of poplar
moonlit deck
backyard lit like prom night
as fireflies strobe
through warm July air
like stars searching
for a place to land

Heart opening
to a more bearable gratitude
swollen tender with hope

pulsing glow
in the palm of my hand

Watermarks

There was a time I snail-carried sorrow
on my back
took all my travels
with that burden masquerading
as home

There were seasons I chased sorrow
down with drink
dissolving the throat lump of loss
with a hundred and one flavours
of oblivion

Sorrow once held me hostage
in the trunk of an old beater
hogtied and ball-gagged
breathing through bullet holes
and trembling
with my heathen prayers

I made my scathed escape
shaking
off the Stockholm syndrome

easing my way back
to the things I know
by heart

Shape Shifter Postscript

What is to give light
must endure burning.

> Viktor Frankl
> *Man's Search for Meaning*

Grief spoken and shared
builds a brilliant bonfire
carries community
with power and purpose

illuminating
our shared humanity
as we give voice
to our songs, our stories

ashes smouldering
in our throats

Sunflowers

Acres of sunflowers, an undulating dawn
golden waves against an azure sky
crowns blown heavenward
then pulled to earth
with the weight of the next generation

A kick, as though on cue, tells me
you're surfing amniotic waves
waiting to shore up in my arms

I already love you too much
I was afraid this would happen

Sitting here in different skin but
somehow more familiar than before
my stomach rises like bread
and I am overcome
with longing

Not sure I'm ready to see the world
through a mother's eyes
to become fluent in the mother tongue

I sing a lullaby for both of us
watch sunflowers glow
cradling newborn faith
in their alchemy of light

Homecoming

This swelling abundance
leaves me breathless

What fluke of fortune
brought you to my breast?
eyelashes tickling my skin

Easing gently
back into my body
this once-abandoned home
a palimpsest
retextured narrative arc

Little one, whose happy hands
patty-cake my neck
how do I serve and protect
your sacred light?

Milk lets down
we melt into one another
nourished and warm

smiling softly
as I rock you
to sleep

Backyard Benediction

I watch you double-fisting dandelions
bare feet dancing the grass thin
your sun-kissed pirouettes
flower crowns
giddy balter among
fierce exuberance
of blooms

Delighting
in every inch of yourself
revelling in your body
and its wondrous work

I'm ripe with gratitude

Your image, a joy-lump
in my throat
arms outstretched
full throttle grin
head in the grass
tiny feet to the sky

kicking out footprints
of light

Customer Service

From somewhere beneath
the cacophony of carts slapped
into submission, shoppers chasing
down the ultimate bargain
the P.A. system announcing
limited time offers
comes the chilling cadence
of your voice

He needs a transplant
Hopefully mine will match

The air is suddenly heavy
with wish-weight
more cumbersome than this
countertop dishwasher bruising
my arms as I stand here
awkwardly queued
tongue thickening in my mouth

We are all so unworthy
of your attention
I watch amazed as you commiserate
over a malfunctioning toaster
with a tight lipped, blue haired broad
who sighs

It's just not all I'd hoped for

How do you manage these transactions
stomach these complaints?

Powerless over my pressure-washed smile
I hand you my receipt, wait
for the gnawing in my stomach
to swallow me whole

An exchange is made,
though not the one I'd hoped for

I step outside, watch leaves quiver
like frightened children

Having returned one gift
I've been given another
burning a hole in the pocket
of my heart

Restless to spend it
I head toward home

Moving Sale

Standing behind the past decade
of our lives spilled onto
plastic covered tables
I wonder
where we kept it all

Uncertain what's ahead
or how it will unfold
emancipated expectation
yielding to possibility
like tulips to the sun

Bittersweet release
of all that's weighed me down
exchanged for coins
from strangers' palms,
carried forth
to some new story

Fragments

1

The butternuts we spread on newspaper
in the basement
the sticky fingered
hammer-wielding glee
of busting shells for
bitter meat
impatient to taste the fruits
of our labor

Giggling, watching shells fly
like shrapnel
delighting in this sanctioned
destruction

such power in our hands

2

Dukes of Hazard Friday nights
Cokes and butter-soaked popcorn
archaic quad-popper quivering
with its bounty
ill-fitting lid vibrating
with energy
it can barely contain

3

Cheating at *Snakes and Ladders*
your doe-eyed innocence
as I'd stealth-slide under the table
folding my scrawny arms
with a scowl

The way you'd coax me back
and sometimes

let me win

4

Hours of Barbies
performing questionable acts
death-defying feats
soap opera mash-up
tabletop dancing
pirouette torpedo

5

Mel's Diner role play
on mom's bingo nights
liberating china
from the dark of the cupboard
messing with the *Weight Watchers* scale

The way you shared the blame
when Flo's *'Kiss my Grits'!*
became too passionate
for the stemware

solidarity under fire

6

Christmas Eves we'd nestle in together
tiptoeing the hall at midnight for a peek
ceramic mice adorning the tree
our names and dates for each year

until there was only mine

7

The way I think of you
when playing with my daughters
chasing fireflies
shadow puppets on the wall
magic lantern replay of the past

the way I feel your light in them
our borders, boundless

What We Keep

We slipped in and out of love
like a pair of old shoes
familiar, close at hand, but
no longer fit for long distance travel

The friction of our efforts chafing
spawning blisters that wouldn't heal
we sank inward
slowly losing our shape

I do not regret the trips made
in those shoes, the calloused memory
of our shared history
even as we both move on
to a better fit

Quarantine 2020

I am making flowers
out of broken things

blues, greens
aquamarines
wispy reeds, grass
that sings

I am making flowers
out of broken things

Seaglass gardens bloom
from years of beachcombed bounty
shored up on sand
where our feet have played
and danced

Mosaic-mind entranced
the future, opaque
Technicolour relics
salt-worn smooth
from journeyed depths unknown
some jagged, sharp
splintered

I consider tossing them
but can't abide such disowning

no exiles
every part has a home

Breathe

Sometimes it is necessary to reteach
a thing its loveliness…
until it flowers again from within.

Galway Kinnell
"Saint Francis and the Sow"

Beginner's mind
brought to the body
your supple words
tender eyes
untorn

Brave explorers
searching borders
while outside, hurricane Fiona howls
snarling storm-wolf
searching out her pack

leaves us untroubled
untouched
your touch, light as pollen
windows rattle
with rain rage

Breathing through
contractions of heart
and mind
feeling both new and known
waiting to see
if you think I'm pretty
on the inside

shelter comes in many forms

We later read of category four
devastation
dissonance
that drives me outside
to find the sky on fire
blistered beauty over
the now-still water

reteaching the earth
its loveliness

Lullaby

Man is born free, and everywhere
he is in chains.

> Rousseau
> *The Social Contract*

Lie you down in the sweet summer grass
feel the sun soft-sweeping your skin
if you *must* analyze, let it be
only the Rorschach of clouds
offer your palms to the clear open air
and let go
of what shadows
your soul
know you are whole
invite yourself home

Get off the freight train
of the mind
join the discourse of trees
sanctuary of boughs
canopied over your fears of

    broken
    defective
    unworthy

Feel the earth hold you
in effortless welcome
root yourself in this moment
this body
and know in your bones
that you belong

Feel the love you've been seeking
in your own luscious heart

Awaken to the breath
nuance of wind

this one precious life
nestled deep in your skin

Notes

"Vertigo," p. 43. certain slant of light. Emily Dickinson, "There's a certain Slant of light."

"Happy Hour," p. 44. *Play the song, Sam.* A paraphrased reference to *Casablanca* Hall B. Wallis movie, 1942. *I have been her kind.* Anne Sexton, "Her Kind."

"Precious Metals," p. 49. *go gentle into that good night.* Dylan Thomas, "Do Not Go Gentle Into that Good Night."

"To Be Continued," p. 51. *Do I dare disturb the universe?* T.S. Eliot "The Love Song of J. Alfred Prufrock." "pair of ragged claws" and "I grow older / I grow older" allusions to language in "The Love Song of J. Alfred Prufrock."

"Cruelest Month," p. 57. T.S. Eliot. *The Wasteland.*

"When I See Her From Here," p. 64. *red in tooth and claw.* Alfred Lord Tennyson. "In Memoriam."

"Higher Learning," p. 73. *why the caged bird sings.* Maya Angelou, "I Know Why the Caged Bird Sings."

"Lullaby," p. 94. *this one precious life.* Mary Oliver, "The Summer Day."

Poems Previously Published

(some in earlier versions)

"The Cruelest Month," e*lm & ampersand*, (April 2020).

"Imaginary Lines" and "Requiem for a Scale," *Sulfur: Laurentian University's Literary Journal*, (August 2017, Vol. VII).

"To Be Continued," *Joypuke III*, (2017).

"Sunday Night Bingo," *Understorey Magazine*, (Winter 2016, Issue 7).

"Daily Bread," "Lakeside Distillations," and an excerpt from "My Sister, My Keeper" (formerly titled "Fragments"), *Peacock Journal*, (November 2016).

"Survival Tips," *Ascent Aspirations: Friday's Poems*, (May 6, 2016).

"Lullaby" (formerly titled "Notes to Self XI"), *Lamp in Hand*, (October 2015).

"Notes to Self III" (formerly titled "Notes to Self V"), *Ascent Aspirations, Anthology: As One Cradles Pain*, (2012).

"Rigor Mortis," "Customer Service," *Ascent Aspirations, Close to Quitting Time: An Anthology Celebrating Work*, (2011).

"A La Carte," *Quills*, (Vol. VII, 2010).

"Notes to Self II," (formerly titled "Notes to Self III"), *Arborealis: A Canadian Anthology of Poetry* The Ontario Poetry Society, (October 2010).

"Good Girl," *Other Voices*, (Spring 2010, Volume 22:2).

"Natural Habitats," *Emerging Stars: A Contest Anthology*,
The Ontario Poetry Society, (May 2010).

"Precious Metals," *Toward the Light: Journal of Reflective
Word and Image*, (Summer 2008).

"Feral" and "What we Keep," *Ascent Aspirations:
Anthology Five*, (2008).

"From Notes to Self," (formerly titled "Notes to Self IV"),
Open Minds Quarterly, (Volume IX, Issue I, Spring 2007).

"Placebo," *Ascent Aspirations: Anthology Four; Borderlines*,
(2007).

"Degrees of Separation," "Gardening Notes" and "Sunflowers,"
Dorothy Sargent Rosenberg Poetry Contest
Published online, (2007).

Acknowledgments

I am beyond grateful for the beautiful people in my life — my beloved family and friends who have supported and encouraged me in painful times, while celebrating my triumphs. Thank you for loving me when I didn't feel lovable, for believing in me when I couldn't believe in myself. I cherish you, my light weavers. I want to extend particular recognition and gratitude to my cousin, Kayte McLaughlin, for more gifts than I could ever hope to mention here, not the least of which is her beautiful cover art contribution to this book.

It is with deep appreciation and respect that I acknowledge the compassionate and highly skilled therapists who have helped support, guide and accompany me in my healing journey. Thank you for holding space and bearing witness. You know who you are. I would also like to extend my gratitude and respect to my fellow warriors in the recovery community. You are fierce and brave. You inspire me.

Warmest appreciation for Keith, Ellen and Brendan Helmuth of Chapel Street Editions for publishing and promoting my work. You are such a treasure to our community. Many thanks to the Writer's Federation of New Brunswick and the Odd Sundays crew for their encouragement and support. Grateful acknowledgement to Allan Hudson and the *South Branch Scribbler*. Special thanks to Kathy Mac and Roger Moore for your generous time and attention in helping me improve my craft.

Very special thanks to Kerry-Lee Powell, for her attentive reading of this collection in its fledgling form while occupying the role of Writer-in-Residence at UNB. Without your kind, sensitive and invaluable feedback, this manuscript would still be collecting dust in my closet. Many thanks to Lee Thompson for your substantial editing expertise and guidance. Thank you to Melanie Craig-Hansford for your valuable feedback at WordSpring's Blue Pencil session.

Warm gratitude to Inbal Bahar and Wanda MacFarlane for being part of our small but mighty writers' circle. Wanda, thank you for your guitar, your gorgeous voice, and the careful time and attention you have devoted to this manuscript with your feedback and reflections. Heartfelt thanks to Jenn Carson and Jane Tims for your friendship, feedback and generous words of praise. Thank you to Bryn Harris, Pat Post, Neil Sampson and so many others in the writing community for your friendship and encouragement. Appreciative acknowledgment to James Arseneau for reading multiple versions of these poems — without complaint — despite poetry not really being his thing.

It is with deepest gratitude and love that I acknowledge my cherished daughters, Sophie and Lily. Words can never express what you mean to me.

And thank you, gentle readers, for spending your time with this book. Thank you to all the beautiful humans with loving heart and lamp in hand who gift the world with compassion, understanding, and kindness, extending grace, care, patience, and accompaniment to the walking wounded. No one should have to walk alone.

About the Author

Michelle McLean is a grateful mother, clinical social worker and addictions counsellor, educator, animal and nature-lover, dreamer, and seeker of treasure in all forms. Her poetry has appeared in a number of publications, including *Quills, elm & ampersand, Ascent Aspirations, Peacock Journal, Understorey, Other Voices, Sulfur,* and *JONAH.* Her collection of children's poetry, *When Pigs Fly and Other Poems,* was published in 2020 by Chapel Street Editions. Her eldest daughter, Sophie Arseneau, is the illustrator and her youngest daughter, Lily Arseneau, is a contributing illustrator. Michelle and her family live in Carlow, New Brunswick.